U.S. Air Force Aviation
A Military Photo Logbook
Volume 1

COMPILED BY
DENNIS R. JENKINS

specialtypress
PUBLISHERS AND WHOLESALERS

ISBN 978-1-58007-113-0

Item Number SP113

39966 Grand Avenue
North Branch, MN 55056 USA
(651) 277-1400 or (800) 895-4585
www.specialtypress.com

Printed in China

Distributed in the UK and Europe by:

Midland Publishing
4 Watling Drive
Hinckley LE10 3EY, England
Tel: 01455 233 747 Fax: 01455 233 737
www.midlandcountiessuperstore.com

On the Cover, Top Left: *05 October 2006, New Mexico – A CV-22 Osprey flies an air-refueling training mission. The CV-22 adds new capability and fills a long-standing U.S. Special Operations Command requirement to conduct long-range infiltration, exfiltration, and resupply missions during night operations.* (U.S. Air Force photo by Tech Sgt. Cecilio M. Ricardo Jr.)

On the Cover, Top Right: *Air Force Chief of Staff General T. Michael Moseley has said that the replacement for the KC-135 Stratotanker, shown here refueling F-15 Eagles, has moved up to the top procurement priority because of its enabling effect on all other strategic capabilities of the Air Force.* (U.S. Air Force photo by Staff Sgt. James L. Harper, Jr.)

On the Cover, Bottom Left: *13 October 2006, Beale AFB, California – Avionics specialists with the 12th Aircraft Maintenance Unit prepare an RQ-4 Global Hawk for a runway taxi test. The Global Hawk is scheduled to begin flying at Beale in early November.* (U.S. Air Force photo by Stacey Knott)

On the Cover, Bottom Right: *10 February 2006, Fort Irwin, California – A C-17 Globemaster III turns around at the end of a dirt runway after landing. The aircraft is from March Air Reserve Base, California.* (U.S. Air Force photo by Tech. Sgt. Joe Zuccaro)

On the Back Cover, Upper Left: *19 January 2006, Cape Canaveral AFS, Florida – An Atlas V carrying the New Horizons probe launches from Space Launch Complex 41 on a nine-year mission to explore Pluto and the edge of the solar system.* (U.S. Air Force photo)

On the Back Cover, Lower Left: *13 January 2006, Andersen AFB, Guam – Airmen conduct a foreign object damage walkdown before a morning sortie during an air expeditionary deployment. These B01B Lancers provide the U.S. Pacific Command a continuous bomber presence.* (U.S. Air Force photo by Master Sgt. Val Gempis)

On the Back Cover, Lower Right: *13 January 2006, Langley AFB, Virginia – Ralph D. Heath, executive vice president of Lockheed Martin's aeronautical division, speaks during the F-22A Raptor's initial operating capability ceremony.* (U.S. Air Force photograph by SrA Austin Knox)

On the Title Page: *10 November 2006, over the Idaho Sawtooth Mountains – A formation of F-15s and an F-16 flies to the Idaho training ranges.* (U.S. Air Force photo by Master Sgt. Kevin J. Gruenwald)

CONTENTS

INTRODUCTION

The United States Air Force has had a worldwide presence since its establishment by the National Security Act of 1947. The year 2006 was no different. Humanitarian missions around the globe, combat operations in Afghanistan and Iraq, and the ever-present training exercises kept the service busy. In addition, three new aircraft came on the scene. The Lockheed Martin F-22 Raptor entered operational service, the Bell V-22 Osprey finally began entering the inventory, and the Lockheed Martin F-35 Lightning II Joint Strike Fighter made its first flight. Additionally, a highly modified Lockheed Martin C-5M Galaxy, intended to extend the airlifter's service past 2020, began its flight test program.

Like all organizations, the Air Force likes to record its accomplishments, and employs a large team of professional photographers as well as many amateurs. These photographers have few restrictions placed on them about what or when they shoot (although many photographs are never released due to security concerns). The images they capture tend to concentrate on people and events because that is the essence of any organization. Nevertheless, the hardware gets its fair share of exposure, and that is the emphasis of this book.

Military photographers or service members took the photographs contained herein and show the Air Force as it exists, in its glory and its sadness, in peace and at war. The captions are edited versions of what the photographer wrote – sometimes I would have emphasized a different aspect of the photograph, but it was not my choice. Often the photographs exist in a vacuum, with little context – there might be a detail shot of a piece of nose art or a weapon with no corresponding overall photo of the aircraft. This is how the Air Force released the photo. Other times, the photos trace a story, for instance of the Lockheed Martin C-5 Galaxy that crashed at Dover AFB, Delaware – there are photos of the crash, and also of the reclamation of the airframe a few months later.

The photographs run the gamut from exciting, action-filled shots of Mach 2 fighters, to pictures of supplies waiting to be loaded onto a transport aircraft, bombers dropping weapons, and helicopters rescuing stranded people, aircraft fresh off the assembly line, and ones older than most of the people who read this book. A few Allies are represented when they participated in joint operations or exercises, and at least one former enemy that got too close.

The 300+ photographs represent a cross-section of the Air Force and what it accomplished during 2006. The photographs are presented in roughly chronological order (a few liberties were taken to allow a clean layout for the book) and attempt to show a balanced view, but that is for the reader to ultimately decide.

Dennis R. Jenkins
Cape Canaveral, Florida

04 January 2006, off the Coast of Virginia – Captain Chris Batterton aggressively banks his Lockheed F-22A Raptor during a basic fighting maneuver training mission over the Atlantic Ocean. The 27th Fighter Squadron of the 1st Fighter Wing is the first operational Air Force unit to fly the Raptor. (U. S. Air Force photo by Tech. Sgt. Ben Bloker)

09 January 2006, Balad Air Base, Iraq – Airmen with Detachment 5, 721st Air Mobility Operations Group, help unload equipment from a Lockheed C-5 Galaxy. The unit deployed from Ramstein Air Base, Germany. (U.S. Air Force photo)

12 January 2006, Keesler AFB, Mississippi – 65-0980 was the last WC-130H to depart Keesler on its way to Willow Grove, Pennsylvania, when the 403rd Wing converted to the Lockheed WC-130J Hercules. (U.S. Air Force photo by Staff Sgt. J. Justin Pearce)

11 January 2006, Andersen AFB, Guam – A Boeing B-52H Stratofortress from Barksdale AFB, Louisiana, sits in Hangar 1 during phase maintenance. The B-52s come here from a forward-deployed location and go into phase maintenance every 300 flying hours. The $34-million hangar is the newest in the Air Force and can house any type of Air Force aircraft. (U.S. Air Force photo by Tech. Sgt. Shane A. Cuomo)

09 January 2006, Kirtland AFB, New Mexico – Members of the 58th Maintenance Squadron use a new aircraft stand to work on a Sikorsky MH-53J Pave Low III helicopter. (U.S. Air Force photo by Damian Bohannon)

11 January 2006, Andersen AFB, Guam – Staff Sgt. Joshua Cormier and Senior Airman Merritt Shaw perform phase maintenance on a Boeing B-52H Stratofortress in Hangar 1. (U.S. Air Force photo by Tech. Sgt. Shane A. Cuomo)

11 January 2006, Andersen AFB, Guam – Airmen conduct a foreign object damage walk on the flightline before a morning sortie. The Airmen, from the 28th Bomb Wing at Ellsworth AFB, South Dakota, are on an air expeditionary deployment. These Boeing B-1B Lancers provide the U.S. Pacific Command a bomber presence in the Asia-Pacific region. (U.S. Air Force photo by Master Sgt. Val Gempis)

11 January 2006, Dyess AFB, Texas – Airmen load inert bombs onto a Boeing B-1B Lancer during an operational readiness exercise with the 7th Maintenance Operations Squadron and the 9th Bomb Squadron. (U.S. Air Force photo by Airman 1st Class Ryan Summers)

11 January 2006, Andersen AFB, Guam – Mechanics from the 28th Aircraft Maintenance Squadron at Ellsworth AFB, South Dakota, lower the weapons bay fuel tank from a Boeing B-1B Lancer during an inspection. (U.S. Air Force photo by Master Sgt. Val Gempis)

13 January 2006, Langley AFB, Virginia – "We did it!" Ralph D. Heath tells the crowd gathered here today at the Lockheed F-22A Raptor's initial operating capability (IOC) ceremony. Mr. Heath is the executive vice president of Lockheed Martin's aeronautical division. The IOC declaration means the Air Force's fifth generation fighter is ready for war. (U.S. Air Force photograph by Sr. Airman Austin Knox)

21 January 2006, Langley AFB, Virginia – A Lockheed Martin F-22A Raptor takes off during an Operation Noble Eagle mission, marking the first time the F-22 participated in the joint services operation. (U.S. Air Force photo by Staff Sgt. Samuel Rogers)

21 January 2006, over Virginia – A Lockheed F-22A Raptor refuels from a Boeing KC-135R Stratotanker as part of the Raptor's first operational mission. The KC-135 is with the 916th Air Refueling Wing. (U.S. Air Force photo by Airman Shane Dunaway)

24 January 2006, Osan AB, South Korea – A Fairchild-Republic/Lockheed A-10 Thunderbolt II returns after flying a training mission supporting exercise Beverly Bulldog 06-01. Exercise scenarios test the base's ability to protect itself from missile attacks or enemy forces. (U.S. Air Force photo by Tech. Sgt. Jeffrey Allen)

19 January 2006, Cape Canaveral AFS, Florida – A Lockheed Martin Atlas V (AV-010) launches the New Horizons probe on a nine-year mission to explore Pluto and the outer edge of the solar system. (U.S. Air Force photo)

30 January 2006, over Nevada – A Lockheed Martin F-16 Fighting Falcon from the 20th Fighter Wing during Red Flag 06-1. More than 85 aircraft flew missions over the Nevada Test and Training Range. (U.S. Air Force photo by Master Sgt. Kevin J. Gruenwald)

31 January 2006, Langley AFB, Virginia – Lockheed Martin F-22 Raptors will provide strike packages better situational awareness when they pull their first Air Expeditionary Force duty sometime during 2007 with the 27th Fighter Squadron at Langley. They will replace the squadron's Boeing F-15C Eagles. (U.S. Air Force photo by Sr. Airman Austin Knox)

01 February 2006, Barksdale AFB, Louisiana – Munitions on display show the full capabilities of the Boeing B-52H Stratofortress. The bomber has been in front-line service for over 50 years. (U.S. Air Force photo by Tech. Sgt. Robert J. Horstman)

01 February 2006, Barksdale AFB, Louisiana – Airman 1st Class Scott LaCoy with the 2nd Munitions Squadron aligns a Mk-82 bomb into position in front of a Boeing B-52H Stratofortress. (U.S. Air Force photo by Tech. Sgt. Robert J. Horstman)

31 January 2006, over Nevada – A Lockheed Martin F-16 Fighting Falcon from the the 64th Aggressor Squadron at Nellis during Red Flag 06-1. Red Flag tests aircrews-war-fighting skills in realistic combat situations. Along with the Air Force, units are participating from the Army, Navy, Marine Corps, United Kingdom, and Australia. (U.S. Air Force photo by Master Sgt. Kevin J. Gruenwald)

05 February 2006, Southwest Asia – Two Airmen from the 746th Expeditionary Airlift Squadron wait near their Lockheed Martin C-130 Hercules from the Niagara Falls Joint Air Reserve Station, New York. (U.S. Air Force photo by Staff Sgt. Joshua Strang)

05 February 2006, Southwest Asia – Lockheed Martin C-130 Hercules from various Air Guard and Reserve units sit on the flight-line at a deployed location in Southwest Asia. (U.S. Air Force photo by Staff Sgt. Joshua Strang)

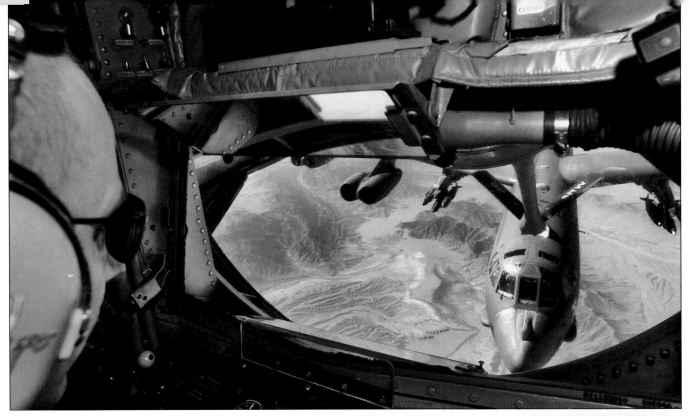

09 February 2006, over Southwest Asia – Tech. Sgt. Thomas Ireland keeps fuel flowing into a Boeing B-52H Stratofortress over Afghanistan during a close-air-support mission. The Boeing KC-135 Stratotanker transfers fuel at about 16 gallons per second. The bomber is from the 2nd Bomb Wing at Barksdale AFB, Louisiana. (U.S. Air Force photo by Master Sgt. Lance Cheung)

08 February 2006, Korat Royal Air Force Base, Thailand – Thai military members watch Maj. Chris Price taxi his Republic-Fairchild/Lockheed A-10 Thunderbolt II during an exercise Cope Tiger '06 mission. Major Price is with the 25th Fighter Squadron at Osan Air Base, South Korea. Some 300 U.S. servicemembers participated in the exercise, about 110 miles northeast of Bangkok, along with an additional 1,000 Thai and Singaporean forces. Cope Tiger provides air-to-air, air-to-ground, and large force employment training for crews while expanding the capabilities and readiness of U.S. and allied forces. (U.S. Air Force photo by Tech. Sgt. Keith Brown)

06 February 2006, C. Moncado Air Base, Honduras – A Lockheed Martin C-5 Galaxy from the 105th Airlift Wing delivered three Sikorsky UH-60L Black Hawks from the New York National Guard's 3-142 Aviation Battalion. (U.S. Air Force photo by Capt. Mike Chillstrom)

08 February 2006, Korat Royal Air Force Base, Thailand – Aircrews from the 25th Fighter Squadron pre-flight several Republic-Fairchild/Lockheed A-10 Thunderbolt IIs before an exercise Cope Tiger '06 mission. (U.S. Air Force photo by Tech. Sgt. Keith Brown)

08 February 2006, Southwest Asia – An F-15E Strike Eagle prepares to refuel while monitoring the battlespace with its targeting pods, a concept known as non-traditional intelligence, surveillance, and reconnaissance. (U.S. Air Force photo by Master Sgt. Lance Cheung)

07 February 2006, Hickam AFB, Hawaii – Boeing F-15C Eagles from the 199th Fighter Squadron of the Hawaii Air National Guard escort the first Hawaii-based C-17 Globemaster III to its home at the 15th Airlift Wing. (U.S. Air Force photo by Tech. Sgt. Shane A. Cuomo)

10 February 2006, Edwards AFB, California – This Lockheed Martin F-16 Fighting Falcon was used for a decontamination test. The aircraft was sprayed with a chemical simulant, washed, then towed to a hangar and heated to 185-degrees to accelerate the weathering of the remaining chemical. (U.S. Air Force photo by Mark McCoy)

10 February 2006, Fort Irwin, California – A Boeing C-17 Globemaster III turns around at the end of a dirt runway after landing during an Army exercise in the desert. The aircraft is from the 452nd Air Mobility Wing at March Air Reserve Base, California. (U.S. Air Force photo by Tech. Sgt. Joe Zuccaro)

14 February 2006, Nellis AFB, Nevada – A Royal Australian Air Force F-111 flies to the ranges during Red Flag 06-1. Australia was one of two international participants in this Red Flag. The RAAF F-111s are due to be retired within the next ten years, marking the end of a 40-year career for the first operational, variable-geometry wing strike fighter. (U.S. Air Force photo by Master Sgt. Kevin J. Gruenwald)

28 February 2006, New York – A crew from the New York Air National Guard's 101st Rescue Squadron at Francis E. Gabreski Field prepares their Sikorsky HH-60 Pave Hawk for a training mission. (U.S. Air Force photo by Master Sgt Jack Braden)

22 February 2006, near Okinawa, Japan – A formation of Boeing F-15 Eagles from the 18th Wing fire AIM-7 Sparrow III missiles against a high-speed target drone as part of a joint service training exercise. The AIM-7 is being phased out of the inventory in favor of the AIM-120 Advanced Medium-Range Air-to-Air Missile (AMRAAM). (U.S. Air Force photo by Tech. Sgt. Richard Freeland)

23 February 2006, Manas Air Base, Kyrgyzstan – A Boeing KC-135 Stratotanker sits on the flightline waiting for crews to de-ice it before it can take off on a refueling mission over Southwest Asia. (U.S. Air Force photo by Staff Sgt. Paul Clifford)

24 February 2006, Whiteman AFB, Missouri – A pilot walks away from an A-10 Thunderbolt II he just delivered to the 442nd Fighter Wing from the 926th Fighter Wing, based near New Orleans. (U.S. Air Force photo by Master Sgt. Bill Huntington)

22 February 2006, New Al Muthana Air Base, Iraq – An Iraqi Air Force C-130E Hercules taxis onto the runway shared by Baghdad International Airport and New Al Muthana Air Base. The aircraft, YI-303 (formerly USAF 63-7826), is one of three cargo aircraft supplied to the Iraqi Air Force by the United States to build the first Iraqi Air Force squadron. (U.S. Air Force photo by Master Sgt. Lance Cheung)

26 February 2006, New Al Muthana Air Base, Iraq – An Iraqi crewmember and Staff Sgt. Dominic Pecoraro (left) watch carefully for enemy weapons fire from their C-130E Hercules. If necessary the loadmasters have flares they can fire away from the aircraft to distract infrared homing missiles such as the SA-7 and Stinger. The Iraqi loadmaster is assigned to the 23rd Squadron, New Al Muthana Air Base, and Sergeant Pecoraro is from the 517th Airlift Squadron at Elmendorf AFB, Alaska. (U.S. Air Force photo by Master Sgt. Lance Cheung)

28 February 2006, Minot AFB, North Dakota – Airmen secure an AGM-129 Advanced Cruise Missile to a Boeing B-52H Stratofortress during an alert generation exercise to test missile loading and aircrew response procedures. (U.S. Air Force photo by Staff Sgt. Jocelyn Rich)

28 February 2006, Minot AFB, North Dakota – An Airman from the 23rd Bomb Squadron removes a window cover on a Boeing B-52H Stratofortress during an alert exercise. (U.S. Air Force photo by Staff Sgt. Jocelyn Rich)

28 February 2006, Minot AFB, North Dakota – Airman 1st Class Michael Schaff secures a B-52H Stratofortress engine intake cover. Airman Schaff is with the 5th Aircraft Maintenance Squadron. (U.S. Air Force photo by Staff Sgt. Jocelyn Rich)

During its first operational combat deployment, the Northrop-Grumman RQ-4 Global Hawk collected nearly 5,000 images of enemy locations, resources, and personnel. (U.S. Air Force photo by Staff Sgt. Christopher Matthews)

01 March 2006, Southwest Asia – With its sensors and ability to gather vast amounts of imagery, the RQ-4 Global Hawk brings a new dimension to intelligence, surveillance, and reconnaissance operations. (U.S. Air Force photo by Staff Sgt. Christopher Matthews)

03 March 2006, Djibouti-Ambouli International Airport, Africa – A U.S. Marine Corps Sikorsky CH-53E Super Stallion helicopter is offloaded from an Air Force Lockheed Martin C-5 Galaxy. (U.S. Air Force photo by Staff Sgt. Nic Raven)

03 March 2006, Langley AFB, Virginia – Maj. Kevin Dolata lands the second Lockheed Martin F-22A Raptor assigned to the 94th Fighter Squadron. The 94th is the second squadron at Langley to receive the new stealth fighter. (U.S. Air Force photo by Airman Vernon Young)

03 March 2006, Langley AFB, Virginia – Lt. Col. Dirk Smith, 94th Fighter Squadron commander, talks with the local media after delivering one of the first two Lockheed Martin F-22A Raptors assigned to the squadron. (U.S. Air Force photo by Tech. Sgt. Ben Bloker)

04 March 2006, near Tucson, Arizona – A World War II-era Republic P-47 Thunderbolt and a Lockheed Martin F-22A Raptor fly in formation during the 2006 Air Combat Command Heritage Conference at Davis-Monthan AFB. (U.S. Air Force photo by Tech. Sgt. Ben Bloker)

04 March 2006, near Tucson, Arizona – Lt. Col. Charles Hainline, an F-4 Phantom pilot from Holloman AFB, New Mexico, and Lt. Col. Michael Shower, an F-22A Raptor pilot from Langley AFB, Virginia, fly in formation. (U.S. Air Force photo by Tech. Sgt. Ben Bloker)

04 March 2006, near Tucson, Arizona – Lt. Col. Michael Shower flies a Lockheed Martin F-22A Raptor during the 2006 Air Combat Command Heritage Conference at Davis-Monthan AFB. (U.S. Air Force photo by Tech. Sgt. Ben Bloker)

04 March 2006, over Tucson, Arizona – The 2006 Air Combat Command Heritage Conference combines different U.S. aircraft representing more than 60 years of aviation history. (U.S. Air Force photo by Airman 1st Class Veronica Pierce)

03 March 2006, Kabul, Afghanistan – Capt. Margarita Correas gives a flight safety brief to Spanish troops before taking off in a Lockheed Martin C-130 Hercules heading for Afghanistan. (U.S. Air Force photo by Staff Sgt. Lara Gale)

08 March 2006, Barksdale AFB, Louisiana – A Boeing B-52H Stratofortress during the Conventional Operational Readiness Exercise. The 2nd Bomb Wing and the 917th Wing participated in the exercise. (U.S. Air Force photo by Master Sgt. Michael A. Kaplan)

08 March 2006, Bagram Air Base, Afghanistan – A U.S. Navy Northrop-Grumman EA-6B Prowler from NAS Whidbey Island, Washington, is prepared for a dawn sortie as part of a joint mission. (U.S. Air Force photo by Master Sgt. Lance Cheung)

08 March 2006, Bagram Air Base, Afghanistan – A Lockheed Martin EC-130H Compass Call from the 41st Expeditionary Electronic Control Squadron (EECS) sits on the flightline as its crew prepares for a night mission. The Compass Call is an airborne tactical weapon system used to deny, degrade, and disrupt the enemy's ability to communicate. Since April 2004, 41st EECS EC-130s have flown more than 700 combat sorties supporting ground forces in Operation Enduring Freedom. (U.S. Air Force photo by Master Sgt. Lance Cheung)

09 March 2006, Southwest Asia – A Lockheed Martin C-5 Galaxy from the Air Force Reserve Command's 433rd Airlift Wing is ready to depart on another mission supporting Operation Iraqi Freedom. (U.S. Air Force photo by Capt. Jeremy Angel)

19 March 2006, Ramstein Air Base, Germany – Two Boeing C-17 Globemaster IIIs taxi on the busy airport ramp while construction of the new 350-room billeting building continues in the background. (U.S. Air Force photo by Master Sgt. John E. Lasky)

09 March 2006, Nellis AFB, Nevada – Capt. Tad Clark and Kenny Schrader, driver of the NASCAR Air Force #21 Wood Brothers Ford Fusion, take off for an orientation flight in a Lockheed Martin F-16 Fighting Falcon from the Thunderbirds aerial demonstration team. Captain Clark is the advance pilot/narrator for the Thunderbirds. (U.S. Air Force photo by Larry McTighe)

13 March 2006, Davis-Monthan AFB, Arizona – Pararescuemen from the 48th Rescue Squadron climb down a rope ladder from a Sikorsky HH-60 Pavehawk, as part of alternate insertion/extraction training. (U.S Air Force photo by Senior Airman Christina Ponte)

13 March 2006, over the Indian Ocean – A Boeing B-52H Stratofortress armed with JDAM GPS-guided bombs refuels while providing close air support to troops on the ground in Afghanistan. (U.S. Air Force photo by Staff Sgt. Doug Nicodemus)

20 March 2006, Kirtland AFB, New Mexico – Airmen prepare to greet Lt. Gen. Michael W. Wooley, commander of the Air Force Special Operations Command, as he delivers the Air Force's first operational Bell CV-22 Osprey to the 58th Special Operations Wing. (U.S. Air Force photo by Staff Sgt. Markus Maier)

20 March 2006, Kirtland AFB, New Mexico – Airmen with the 58th Special Operations Wing hold a banner welcoming the Air Force's first operational Bell CV-22 Osprey. (U.S. Air Force photo by Staff Sgt. Markus Maier)

21 March 2006, Keesler AFB, Mississippi – A new wash system installed by the 403rd Wing blasts a Lockheed Martin C-130J Hercules with 2,000 gallons of water per minute from its 40 nozzles. (U.S. Air Force photo by Tech Sgt. Jame Pritchett)

23 March 2006, Davis-Monthan AFB, Arizona – A Fairchild-Republic/Lockheed A-10 Thunderbolt II armed with training AGM-65 Mavericks and an ECM pod takes part in the 2006 Hawgsmoke competition. The Warthog has been in operational service for 30 years, and recent upgrades ensure its continued effectiveness for at least another decade. (U.S. Air Force photo)

23 March 2006, Davis-Monthan AFB, Arizona – Hawgsmoke is a biennial bombing and tactical gunnery competition of the A-10, in which 20 squadrons worldwide come together and compete for the honor of the "Best of the Best" in ground attack and target destruction. (U.S. Air Force photo by Airman 1st Class Jesse Shipps)

23 March 2006, Gila Bend Air Force Auxiliary Field, Arizona – An A-10 Thunderbolt II fires its 30-mm GAU-8 cannon at the Barry Goldwater Range near Tucson. Each A-10 team has four members with 100 rounds each to use toward the target. (U.S. Air Force photo by Senior Airman Christina D. Ponte)

23 March 2006, Gila Bend Air Force Auxiliary Field, Arizona – This A-10 banks around the tower after it fired its 30-mm cannon. (U.S. Air Force photo by Senior Airman Christina D. Ponte)

23 March 2006, Davis-Monthan AFB, Arizona – This A-10 Thunderbolt II shows off the muzzle for the 30-mm GAU-8 cannon. (U.S. Air Force photo by Airman 1st Class Jesse Shipps)

23 March 2006, Gila Bend Air Force Auxiliary Field, Arizona – The Barry-Goldwater Range, formerly known as the Gila Bend Gunnery Range, is located in Southern Arizona, not far from Tucson and Davis-Monthan AFB. It is also frequently used by squadrons based at Luke AFB in Phoenix. (U.S. Air Force photo by Senior Airman Christina D. Ponte)

30 March 2006, off the coast of Virginia – Lt. Col. Bryan Turner and Maj. Thomas McAtee fly in formation with Lt. Col. Wade Tolliver during a training mission. Colonel Turner and Major McAtee are F-16 pilots assigned to the Virginia ANG's 149th Fighter Squadron at Sandstone, Virginia. Colonel Tolliver is an F-22A Raptor pilot with the 27th Fighter Squadron at Langley. The Virginia Air National Guard is currently transitioning to the new Lockheed Martin F-22A Raptor and will replace the F-16 Fighting Falcons as early as October 2007. (U.S. Air Force photo by Tech. Sgt. Ben Bloker)

27 March 2006, Ramstein Air Base, Germany – A rainbow appears over a Lockheed Martin C-130 Hercules and the air traffic control tower at Ramstein. The aircraft belongs to the 187th Airlift Squadron of the Wyoming Air National Guard in Cheyenne. (U.S. Air Force photo by Master Sgt. John E. Lasky)

03 April 2006, Dover AFB, Delaware – A Lockheed Martin C-5B Galaxy (84-0059) crashed a mile short of the runway after having to shut down the No. 2 engine shortly after takeoff. The subsequent investigation found that the pilots and flight engineers did not properly configure, maneuver, and power the aircraft during approach and landing. Following a normal takeoff and initial climb, the C-5 aircrew observed a No. 2 engine "thrust reverser not locked" indication light. They shut down the No. 2 engine as a precaution and initiated a return to Dover. The board determined that during the return to the base the pilots and flight engineers continued to use the shut-down No. 2 engine's throttle while leaving the fully-operational No. 3 engine in idle. In addition, both instructor and primary flight engineers failed to brief, and pilots failed to consider and use, a proper flap setting. The pilots' attempt at a visual approach to runway 32 resulted in the aircraft descending well below a normal glidepath for an instrument-aided approach or the normal visual flight rules pattern altitude. All 17 people on board the C-5 survived the crash, but three crewmembers were seriously injured when the aircraft stalled, hit a utility pole, and crashed into a field about a mile short of the runway. The other passengers and crewmembers sustained minor injures and were treated and released from local hospitals. The aircraft was assigned to the 436th Airlift Wing and was flown by members of the 512th Airlift Wing, a Reserve unit at Dover. The C-5 was bound for Ramstein Air Base, Germany, and was carrying 105,000 pounds of replenishment supplies for the U.S. Central Command. The aircraft had been one of the first to receive a "glass cockpit" upgrade under the C-5 Avionics Modernization Program (AMP), but the board determined this played no part in the accident. (U.S. Air Force photos by Doug Curran)

05 April 2006, Southwest Asia – A maintainer with the 379th Expeditionary Aircraft Maintenance Squadron inspects the engine of a Boeing F-15E Strike Eagle at a forward-deployed location. (U.S. Air Force photo by Staff Sgt. Joshua Strang)

03 April 2006, Shaw AFB, South Carolina – Master Sgt. Scott Laws, with the 20th Component Maintenance Squadron, inspects a shut-off valve on an Lockheed Martin F-16 Fighting Falcon. Sergeant Laws made a suggestion that could save the Air Force $320,000 a year by replacing the valve's heat shield instead of the entire valve assembly. (U.S. Air Force photo by Tech. Sgt. Kevin Williams)

04 April 2006, Kenya – Senior Airman Chris Sutton and Master Sgt. Ramon Feliciano help unload humanitarian supplies from a C-130 Hercules in Kenya. The humanitarian effort is part of the Combined Joint Task Force Horn of Africa Flex mission. Airman Sutton is a crew chief and Sergeant Feliciano is a loadmaster with the 746th Air Expeditionary Wing. (U.S. Air Force photo by Maj. Ann P. Knabe)

11 April 2006, over Southwest Asia – Capt. Brian Temple (left) and 1st Lt. Chris Reid of the 340th Expeditionary Air Refueling Squadron fly their Boeing KC-135 Stratotanker during an aerial refueling mission. (U.S. Air Force photo by Staff Sgt. Joshua Strang)

07 April 2006, Scott AFB, Illinois – Bill Murphy marshals a Lockheed Martin C-141C Starlifter from the 445th Airlift Wing. The aircraft, tail number 67-0166, made its final flight and will take its place among other Air Mobility Command aircraft at the heritage airpark being built this year. Murphy is with the 375th Airlift Wing's transient alert section. The 445th, based at Wright-Patterson AFB, Ohio, is converting from the C-141 to the Lockheed Martin C-5 Galaxy. (U.S. Air Force photo by Staff Sgt. Tony R. Tolley)

12 April 2006, over Southwest Asia – A Boeing F-15E Strike Eagle soars over the mountains of Afghanistan in support of Operation Mountain Lion. The crew and fighter are deployed to the 336th Expeditionary Fighter Squadron from the 4th Fighter Wing at Seymour Johnson AFB, North Carolina. (U.S. Air Force photos by Master Sgt. Lance Cheung)

14 April 2006, over Tucson, Arizona – Three Fairchild-Republic/Lockheed-10 Thunderbolt IIs wait to receive an air refueling from a Boeing KC-135E Stratotanker as part of a training mission. The A-10s are assigned to the 358th Fighter Squadron at Davis-Monthan AFB. (U.S. Air Force photo by Senior Airman Christina D. Ponte)

17 April 2006, Edwards AFB, California – Tech. Sgt. Rick Fujimoto makes an adjustment on the engine of an Iraqi Air Force Comp Air 7SLX. Sergeant Fujimoto is with the 653rd Combat Logistics Support Squadron at Robins AFB, Georgia, and one of four crew chiefs on the project. (U.S. Air Force photo by Jet Fabara)

18 April 2006, Edwards AFB, California – A Lockheed Martin F-16 Fighting Falcon carries an AN/AAQ-28(V) LITENING-AT precision targeting pod during tests by the 416th Flight Test Squadron. The LITENING-AT includes a video downlink transmitter currently used in the Predator UAV. (Northrop-Grumman photo via the U.S. Air Force)

17 April 2006, Andersen AFB, Guam – Senior Airman Alex Berger inflates a recently installed nose landing-gear tire on a Boeing B-1B Lancer while Senior Airman Thomas Feenstra prepares to replace the other tire. The airmen are assigned to the 36th Expeditionary Aircraft Maintenance Squadron. (U.S. Air Force photo by Airman 1st Class Michael Dorus)

17 April 2006, Andersen AFB, Guam – Airman 1st Class Francis Pacheco performs maintenance on avionics equipment in the nose of a Boeing B-1B Lancer. (U.S. Air Force photo by Airman 1st Class Michael Dorus)

17 April 2006, Ellsworth AFB, South Dakota – Staff Sgt. Zachariah Ellis performs a structural maintenance inspection on a Boeing B-1B Lancer. Sergeant Ellis is with the 28th Maintenance Squadron. (U.S. Air Force photo by Airman 1st Class Melissa Flores)

18 April 2006, Eielson AFB, Alaska – Lockheed Martin F-16 Fighting Falcons from the 64th Aggressor Squadron at Nellis AFB line up at Eielson for Red Flag-Alaska. The exercise, formerly known as Cope Thunder, provides joint offensive counter-air, interdiction, close-air support, and large-force employment training in a simulated combat environment. (U.S. Air Force photo by Airman 1st Class Justin Weaver)

19 April 2006, Sather Air Base, Iraq – An Air Force Reserve Lockheed Martin C-130 Hercules from the 302nd Airlift Wing at Peterson AFB, Colorado, is readied for takeoff in support of Operation Iraqi Freedom. (U.S. Air Force photo by Master Sgt. Lance Cheung)

20 April 2006, Cape Canaveral AFS, Florida – A Lockheed Martin Atlas V booster lifts off from Space Launch Complex 41 carrying a commercial television satellite into orbit. (Lockheed Martin Corporation photo by Pat Corkery)

09 April 2006, Hill AFB, Utah – A Lockheed Martin F-22A Raptor arrives for minor modifications. Members of the 309th Maintenance Wing will modify 18 F-22s at the Ogden Air Logistics Center at Hill. (U.S. Air Force photo by Bill Orndorf)

20 April 2006, Dover AFB, Delaware – The crew compartment of the Lockheed Martin C-5 Galaxy that crashed on 3 April 2006 is removed from the fuselage. The compartment is expected to be used as a training simulator. (U.S. Air Force photo by Jason Minto)

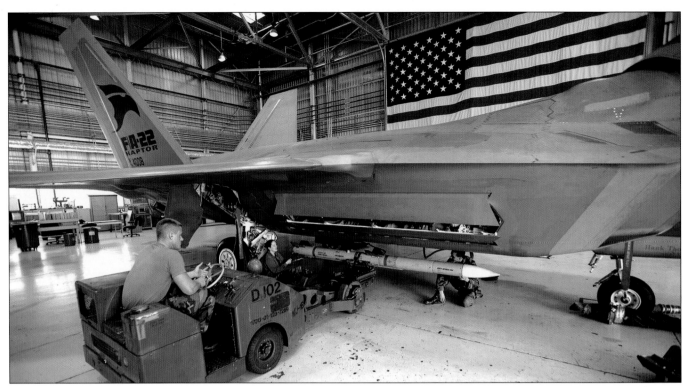

21 April 2006, Edwards AFB, California – Senior Airman Daniel Myers and Staff Sgts. Daphne Jaehn and John Davenport load an AIM-120D Advanced Medium Range Air-to-Air Missile on a Lockheed Martin F-22A Raptor in preparation for noise and vibration testing. The Airmen are assigned to the 412th Aircraft Maintenance Squadron and are with the F-22 Combined Test Force. (U.S. Air Force photo by Kevin Robertson)

21 April 2006, Eielson AFB, Alaska – Lockheed Martin F-16 Fighting Falcons from the 63rd Fighter Squadron at Luke AFB and the 64th Aggressor Squadron at Nellis AFB on the flightline at Eielson for Red Flag-Alaska 06-2. The exercise, previously called Cope Thunder, was enhanced to provide training on the same level as Red Flag at Nellis. (U.S. Air Force photo by Tech. Sgt. Sara Hilmoe)

28 April 2006, Elmendorf AFB, Alaska – Master Sgt. Brad Cooper loads container delivery systems onto a Lockheed Martin C-130 Hercules as part of Red Flag-Alaska 06-2. Cooper is with the 96th Airlift Squadron at Minneapolis-St. Paul Joint Air Reserve Station, Minnesota. (U.S. Air Force photo by Sr. Airman Garrett Hothan)

24 April 2006, Eielson AFB, Alaska – Boeing B-52H Stratofortresses from the 93rd Bomb Squadron at Barksdale AFB, Louisiana, participated in Red Flag-Alaska 06-2. An F-16 takes off in the background. (U.S. Air Force photo by Tech. Sgt. Jeff Walston)

25 April 2006, Eielson AFB, Alaska – A Lockheed Martin F-16 Fighting Falcon from the Air National Guard's 175th Fighter Squadron at Sioux Falls during Red Flag-Alaska 06-2. (U.S. Air Force photo by Tech. Sgt. Jeff Walston)

28 April 2006, over South Korea – A formation of Lockheed Martin F-16 Fighting Falcons from the 8th Fighter Wing from Kunsan Air Base, South Korea, is led by Col. Brian Bishop, 8th FW commander (flying solo at lower right). (U.S. Air Force photo by Master Sgt. Richard Freeland)

U.S. Air Force Aviation

29 April 2006, Willow Grove ARS, Pennsylvania – Tech. Sgts. Bruce Hart (left) and Scott Edsell secure an AGM-65 Maverick missile to a Fairchild-Republic/Lockheed A-10 Thunderbolt II during the first phase of an operational readiness inspection at the Willow Grove Air Reserve Station. Sergeants Hart and Edsell are with the Pennsylvania Air National Guard's 111th Maintenance Squadron. (U.S. Air Force photo by Staff Sgt. Marie Harmon)

29 April 2006, Willow Grove ARS, Pennsylvania – Senior Airman Stephen Close with the 111th Maintenance Squadron secures rocket pods during an operational readiness inspection. (U.S. Air Force photo by Staff Sgt. Marie Harmon)

28 April 2006, Eielson AFB, Alaska – An A-10 Thunderbolt II strafes a "hostile" convoy at the bombing range during Red Flag-Alaska 06-2. The A-10 is from the 75th Fighter Squadron at Pope AFB, North Carolina. (U.S. Air Force photo by Tech. Sgt. Jeff Walston)

30 April 2006, Andersen AFB, Guam – A Northrop-Grumman B-2 Spirit lands to replace a Boeing B-1B Lancer at Andersen as part of the continuous bomber rotation. (U.S. Air Force photo by Airman 1st Class Michael S. Dorus)

03 May 2006, Southwest Asia – A Boeing B-52H Stratofortress is on its way to a combat mission over Afghanistan in support of Operation Enduring Freedom. (U.S. Air Force photo by Senior Master Sgt. John Rohrer)

30 April 2006, Edwards AFB, California – A parachute extracts a Type 5 heavy pallet from the back of a Lockheed Martin C-130J Hercules during air-drop certification tests (U.S. Air Force photo by Tech. Sgt. Dave Buttner)

01 May 2006, Dover AFB, Delaware – A recovery team salvages cargo from the Lockheed Martin C-5 Galaxy that crashed at Dover on April 3. Undamaged cargo was sent on to its final destination. (U.S. Air Force photo by Doug Curran)

05 May 2006, Robins AFB, Georgia – Monroe Allen (left) and Jessie Walker tear down a Lockheed Martin C-5 Galaxy main landing gear at the Warner Robins Air Logistics Center. (U.S. Air Force photo by James Morrow)

04 May 2006, Balad Air Base, Iraq – Three contract maintainers walk a General Atomics RQ-1 Predator unmanned aerial vehicle into a shelter. They are assigned to the 46th Expeditionary Aircraft Maintenance Unit. (U.S. Air Force photo by Airman 1st Class Jason Ridder)

05 May 2006, Wright-Patterson AFB, Ohio – Families swarm to greet former prisoners of war in the Lockheed Martin C-141 Starlifter named "Hanoi Taxi" when it arrived at the National Museum of the United States Air Force after its retirement ceremony. The "Hanoi Taxi" was the first aircraft to arrive in Hanoi in February 1973 to pick up POWs returning to the United States. It is now on public display at the museum. (U.S. Air Force photo by Tech. Sgt. Larry A. Simmons)

04 May 2006, Eielson AFB, Alaska – Two of three aggressor paint schemes are displayed on F-16 Fighting Falcons participating in Red Flag-Alaska. The F-16s are from the 64th Aggressor Squadron at **Nellis AFB.** (U.S. Air Force photo by Master Sgt. Rob Wieland)

07 May 2006, over Iraq – An F-16 flies past the window of 1st Lt. Justin Hargrove after refueling with the KC-135. Hargrove is deployed to the 340th Expeditionary Air Refueling Squadron. (U.S. Air Force photo by Senior Airman Brian Ferguson)

08 May 2006, New Al Muthana Air Base, Iraq – A maintainer walks to secure an Iraqi Air Force C-130E Hercules during a sand storm that engulfed the Baghdad area and caused near-zero visibility. (U.S. Air Force photo by Staff Sgt. Jason Serrit)

09 May 2006, Mojave, California – The Scaled Composites Proteus carries the pod that eventually will contain the radar to be used on the Global Hawk unmanned aerial vehicle. A year of testing will begin in September once the radar is installed. (U.S. Air Force photo)

08 May 2006, Alpena, Michigan – A Boeing C-17 Globemaster III from McChord AFB, Washington, sits on the tarmac at Alpena during Exercise Thunderbolt. (U.S. Air Force photo by Airman 1st Class Chad M. Kellum)

09 May 2006, Tyndall AFB, Florida – A weapons loading team led by Staff Sgt. Roderick Abad attach an AIM-7M Sparrow missile into position on a Boeing F-15 Eagle during a weapon systems evaluation. The AIM-7 missile is being phased out of the Air Force inventory in favor of the AIM-120 AMRAAM. (U.S. Air Force photo by Tech. Sgt. Ben Bloker)

11 May 2006, over the Gulf of Tadjoura in Djibouti, Africa – Air Force pararescuemen from the 304th Expeditionary Rescue Squadron free-fall during a high-altitude jump. (U.S. Navy photo by Photographer's Mate 2nd Class Scott Taylor)

12 May 2006, Ramstein Air Base, Germany – Maintainers from the 723rd Air Mobility Squadron mount an engine on a Lockheed Martin C-5 Galaxy. (U.S. Air Force photos by Master Sgt. John E. Lasky)

14 May 2006, Southwest Asia – A Royal Air Force Tornado GR4 takes on fuel from a Boeing KC-135 Stratotanker. The Tornado and crew are from 617 Squadron at RAF Lossiemouth, England. The KC-135 and crew are deployed to the 340th Expeditionary Air Refueling Squadron from the 905th Air Refueling Squadron at Grand Forks AFB, North Dakota. (U.S. Air Force photo by Master Sgt. Lance Cheung)

13 May 2006, Robins AFB, Georgia – Airmen from the United States Air Force Air Demonstration Squadron, the Thunderbirds, line up to form the number 4,000 to commemorate the team's milestone air show. (U.S. Air Force photo)

16 May 2006, Balad Air Base, Iraq – Joseph Stutzman and Robert Attard, contractors from General Atomics Aeronautical Systems switch an AGM-114 Hellfire missile from one MQ-1 Predator to another. Mr. Stutzman and Mr. Attard are aircraft mechanics assigned to the 46th Expeditionary Aircraft Maintenance Unit. Contractors began replacing some military maintainers in February 2006, and recently took over as the primary mechanics for the Predator. (U.S. Air Force photo by Senior Airman Brian Ferguson)

16 May 2006, Deridder, Louisiana – A Fairchild-Republic/Lockheed A-10 Thunderbolt II from Barksdale AFB rolls onto a target after being called in by a joint terminal air controller during urban combat air support training. The training took place in Deridder, where the 458th Combat Training Squadron from nearby Fort Polk has an agreement that allows flights over the city for more realistic urban conditions. The A-10 is unarmed except for training shapes. (U.S. Air Force Photo by Master Sgt. Jack Braden)

16 May 2006, Balad Air Base, Iraq – Lightning strikes near the control tower and a C-130 Hercules. Balad handles more than 750 cargo flights monthly, and is the Department of Defense's busiest single runway. (U.S. Air Force photo by Senior Airman James Croxon)

16 May 2006, over the Atlantic Ocean – A Boeing C-17 Globemaster III from the 14th Airlift Squadron, Charleston AFB flies off after releasing flares. The "smoke angel" is caused the vortex from the engines. (U.S. Air Force photo by Tech. Sgt. Russell E. Cooley IV)

17 May 2006, Marietta, Georgia – Air Force and congressional dignitaries along with local attendees are on hand to celebrate the completion of the first of 111 Galaxies that will be modified into C-5Ms. (Lockheed Martin Corporation photo)

16 May 2006, over Hawaii – An extraction chute opens over the drop zone during an airdrop training mission with Boeing C-17 Globemaster IIIs from the 535th Airlift Squadron, Hickam AFB, Hawaii. (U.S. Air Force photo by Tech. Sgt. Shane A. Cuomo)

20 May 2006, Andrews AFB, Maryland – The three-day 56th annual Department of Defense 2006 Joint Service Open House highlighted American aviators, aircraft, and technology. (U.S. Air Force photo by Senior Airman Jeff Andrejcik)

23 May 2006, Bagram Air Base, Afghanistan – A Fairchild-Republic/Lockheed A-10 Thunderbolt II takes off on a combat mission in support of Operation Enduring Freedom. The A-10 is deployed from the Air Force Reserve Command's 442nd Fighter Wing at Whiteman AFB, Missouri. (U.S. Air Force photo by Maj. David Kurle)

23 May 2006, over Alaska – Lockheed Martin F-22s from the 1st Fighter Wing stationed at Langley AFB fly to Elmendorf AFB, Alaska. The 7.5 hour transit was the longest continuous deployment of F-22s to-date, as 12 Raptors transited to participate in Exercise Northern Edge. (Photo by Paul Weatherman)

23 May 2006, Elmendorf AFB, Alaska – A Lockheed Martin F-22 Raptor from the 27th Fighter Squadron lands at Elmendorf to participate in Exercise Northern Edge 2006. The Air Force selected Elmendorf as the home for the next operational F-22 wing, with the first of 36 Raptors expected in fall 2007. (U.S. Air Force photo by Tech. Sgt. Keith Brown)

26 May 2006, Holloman AFB, New Mexico – *Two Bell CV-22 Ospreys prepare to land while taking part in the filming of the movie "Transformers." These Osprey are two of only three CV-22s in the Air Force inventory.* (U.S. Air Force photo by Airman 1st Class Russell Scalf)

23 May 2006, Ellsworth AFB, South Dakota – Boeing B-1B Lancers participate in Exercise Badlands Express to prepare for an operational readiness inspection in July. Note the intake covers on the B-1B on the facing page. (U.S. Air Force photo by Senior Airman Michael B. Keller)

28 May 2006, South Pacific – This Boeing C-17 Globemaster III crew views Guadalcanal during take-off from Honiara International Airport, Solomon Islands. Two C-17s from the 15th Airlift Wing and Hawaii Air National Guard's 154th Wing at Hickam AFB, Hawaii, are helping the Australian Defense Force reposition its forces from the Solomon Islands back to Australia to better support peace operations in East Timor. (U.S. Air Force photo by Tech. Sgt. Shane A. Cuomo)

28 May 2006, Honiara International Airport, Solomon Islands – Airmen from the Australian 1st Air Terminal Squadron observe the loading of equipment onto a Boeing C-17 Globemaster III. (U.S. Air Force photo by Tech. Sgt. Shane A. Cuomo)

30 May 2006, RAAF Townsville, Australia – Airman James Ngo marshals a second armored personnel carrier onto a C-17 Globemaster III at Royal Australian Air Force Base Townsville. (U.S. Air Force photo by Tech. Sgt. Shane A. Cuomo)

30 May 2006, over the Pacific Ocean – A Northrop-Grumman B-2 Spirit from the 509th Bomb Wing at Whiteman AFB soars after a refueling mission as part of a continuous bomber presence in the Asia-Pacific region. (U.S. Air Force photo by Staff Sgt. Bennie J. Davis III)

06 June 2006, Eielson AFB, Alaska – Lockheed Martin F-16 Fighting Falcons from the Iowa and Ohio Air National Guard participate in Exercise Northern Edge 2006. The joint training exercise hosted by Alaskan Command is one of a series of U.S. Pacific Command exercises that prepare joint forces to respond to crises in the Asian Pacific region. (U.S. Air Force photo by Staff Sgt. Joshua Strang)

06 June 2006, Fort Wainwright, Alaska – Airmen from the 31st Rescue Squadron at Kadena Air Base, Japan, load a patient onto an Sikorsky HH-60 Pave Hawk during exercise Northern Edge 2006. (U.S. Air Force Photo by Staff Sgt Joshua Strang)

06 June 2006, Eielson AFB, Alaska – Three Lockheed Martin F-16 Fighting Falcons from the Iowa Air National Guard's 132nd Fighter Squadron display their tail art during exercise Northern Edge 2006. (U.S. Air Force Photo by Staff Sgt Joshua Strang)

06 June 2006, Eielson AFB, Alaska – Lockheed Martin F-16 Fighting Falcons aggressor aircraft from Nellis AFB also participated in Exercise Northern Edge 2006. The F-16s have recently been joined by a squadron of Boeing F-15 Eagle aggressors painted in similar camouflage paint schemes. (U.S. Air Force photo by Staff Sgt. Joshua Strang)

08 June 2006, Ellsworth AFB, South Dakota – A Boeing B-1 Lancer heads for the runway while another takes off. The aircraft are assigned to the 28th Bomb Wing. (U.S Air Force photo by Airman 1st Class Angela Ruiz)

09 June 2006, Eielson AFB, Alaska – A Lockheed Martin F-16 Fighting Falcon from the Ohio Air National Guard's 180th Fighter Wing drops a flare while performing maneuvers at Exercise Northern Edge 2006. (U.S. Air Force photo by Master Sgt. Rob Wieland)

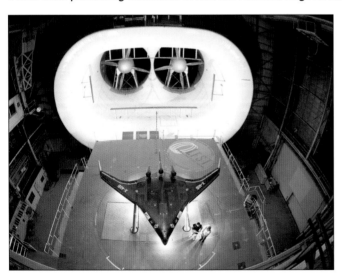

13 June 2006, Langley, Virginia – Researchers are testing a 21-foot wingspan prototype of the blended wing-body Boeing X-48B in the full-scale wind tunnel at the NASA Langley Research Center. The Air Force Research Laboratory partnered with Boeing Phantom Works and the National Aeronautics and Space Administration to study the structural, aerodynamic, and operational advantages of the advanced aircraft concept. (NASA photo by Jeff Captain)

10 June 2006, over San Antonio, Texas – The Beech T-1A Jayhawk is a medium-range, twin-engine jet trainer used in the advanced phase of specialized undergraduate pilot training for students selected to fly airlift or tanker aircraft. It is also used to support navigator training for the U.S. Air Force, Navy, Marine Corps, and international services. These T-1As are on a training mission near Randolph AFB, Texas. (U.S. Air Force photo by Lt. Col. Russell Hopkinson)

12 June 2006, RAF Lakenheath, England – Airmen help unload an Sikorsky HH-60G Pave Hawk helicopter from a Boeing C-17 Globemaster III. The helicopters are being reassigned to RAF Lakenheath from Naval Air Station Keflavik, Iceland. (U.S. Air Force photo)

14 June 2006, Bagram Air Base, Afghanistan – Col. Tony Johnson takes off in a Fairchild-Republic/Lockheed A-10 Thunderbolt II for a combat mission in Afghanistan. Colonel Johnson is deployed from Whiteman AFB, Missouri, where he commands the 442nd Operations Group. He is serving as the commander of the 455th Expeditionary Operations Group while at Bagram. (U.S. Air Force photo by Maj. David Kurle)

14 June 2006, Southwest Asia – Firefighters from the 386th Expeditionary Civil Engineer Squadron at a deployed location in Southwest Asia. (U.S. Air Force photo by Staff Sgt. Ryan Hansen)

14 June 2006, Portland, Oregon – A Boeing F-15 Eagle from the 142nd Fighter Wing takes off from the Portland Air National Guard Base during an operational readiness inspection. (U.S. Air Force photo by Senior Airman John Hughel)

17 June 2006, near Lake Mead, Arizona – An EC-130H Compass Call flies a training mission. These modified Lockheed Martin C-130 Hercules perform tactical command, control, and communications countermeasures. (U.S. Air Force photo)

20 June 2006, over Southern California – Marine Maj. David Montesano guides his CH 53E Super Stallion helicopter while taking on fuel from an HC-130 assigned to the 79th Rescue Squadron at Davis-Monthan AFB. (U.S. Air Force photo by Airman 1st Class Veronica Pierce)

18 June 2006, over Florida – Capt. Joseph Drummond from the 55th Fighter Squadron participates in Combat Archer at Tyndall AFB. Approximately 145 personnel from Shaw AFB participated in the exercise. (U.S. Air Force photo by Lt. Col. Clyde Cooper)

19 June 2006, over Georgia – A modernized Lockheed Martin C-5M Galaxy makes its maiden flight at Dobbins Air Reserve Base. Upgrades to the venerable airlifter include more powerful General Electric CF6-80C2 commercial engines, a modern cockpit with a digital flight control system, a new communications suite, and enhanced navigation and safety equipment. (Lockheed Martin photos)

18 June 2006, Pacific Ocean – A Northrop-Grumman B-2 Spirit and 16 other aircraft from the Air Force, Navy, and Marine Corps fly over the USS Kitty Hawk (CV-63), USS Ronald Reagan (CVN-76), and USS Abraham Lincoln (CVN-72) carrier strike groups in the western Pacific Ocean to kick off Exercise Valiant Shield 2006. The joint exercise consists of 28 naval vessels, more than 300 aircraft, and approximately 20,000 servicemembers. (U.S. Navy photo by Chief Photographer's Mate Todd P. Cichonowicz)

21 June 2006, Andersen AFB, Guam – Staff Sgt. Michael Hinton climbs into a Boeing KC-10 Extender during Valiant Shield. Sergeant Hinton is a boom operator with the 9th Air Refueling Squadron at Travis AFB. (U.S. Air Force photo by Tech. Sgt. Shane A. Cuomo)

22 June 2006, Nellis AFB, Nevada – a pair of General Atomics RQ-1 Predator unmanned aerial vehicles (UAV) practice landings and take-offs prior to a deployment to Southwest Asia. (U.S. Air Force Photo by MSgt Robert W. Valenca)

21 June 2006, Nellis AFB, Nevada – The 65th Aggressor Squadron at Nellis recently began flying the Boeing F-15 Eagle, supplementing the Lockheed Martin F-16 Fighting Falcon aggressors flown by the 64th Aggressor Squadron. (U.S. Air Force photo)

20 June 2006, Hickam AFB, Hawaii – A pilot from the 99th Reconnaissance Squadron at Beale AFB walks to his Lockheed Martin U-2S Dragon Lady, en route to South Korea. The U-2s are undergoing a $1.5 billion cockpit upgrade that replaces the existing cockpit instruments with state-of-the-art, touch-screen technology. (U.S. Air Force photo by Tech. Sgt. Shane A. Cuomo)

20 June 2006, Osan Air Base, South Korea – Lt. Col. Lars Hoffman reviews his checklist before flying the newly-modified Block 20 Lockheed Martin U-2S Dragon Lady on its first flight from Osan. All U-2S models were originally delivered as U-2Rs or TR-1As. Colonel Hoffman is the commander of the 5th Reconnaissance Squadron. (U.S. Air Force photo by Staff Sgt. Andrea Knudson)

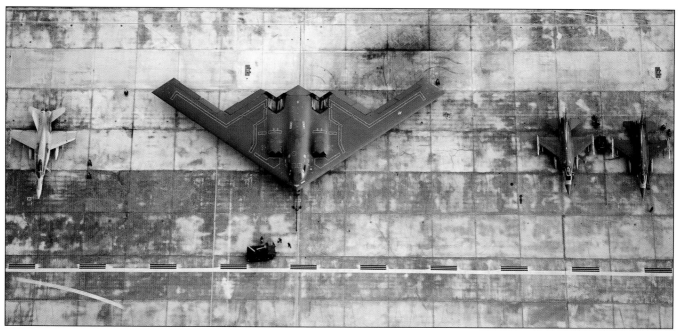

22 June 2006, Andersen AFB, Guam – A Northrop-Grumman B-2 Spirit, two Lockheed Martin F-16 Fighting Falcons, and a Navy Boeing F/A-18 Hornet sit on the flightline during Exercise Valiant Shield. (U.S. Air Force photo by Staff Sgt. Bennie J. Davis III)

20 June 2006, Osan Air Base, South Korea – An improved U-2S Dragon Lady, taxis to the runway followed by a high-performance Chevrolet Camaro Z28 chase car. Osan AB was the last forward operating location to receive the new Block 20 aircraft. (U.S. Air Force photo by Staff Sgt. Andrea Knudson)

20 June 2006, Osan Air Base, South Korea – Maj. Michael Clavenna returns to Osan Air Force Base, South Korea, from the last operational reconnaissance flight in the Block 10 U-2S. Major Clavenna is the assistant director of operations for the 5th Reconnaissance Squadron. (U.S. Air Force photo by Staff Sgt. Andrea Knudson)

26 June 2006, Ellsworth AFB, South Dakota – Above, Senior Airman Ryan McGlocklin (left) and Airman 1st Class Eric Mansfield prepare to load a training bomb into the weapons bay of a Boeing B-1B Lancer. The base was conducting Exercise Badlands Express 06-04 to prepare for an operational readiness inspection in July. Below, Senior Airman Ryan McGlocklin directs a bomb loader into position underneath a training bomb. The Airmen are assigned to the 28th Aircraft Maintenance Squadron. (U.S. Air Force photo by Senior Airman Michael B. Keller)

28 June 2006, Southwest Asia – Maintainers from the Japan Air Self-Defense Force's Iraq Reconstruction Support Airlift Wing tow one of their Lockheed Martin C-130 Hercules from the flightline at a forward operating base. (U.S. Air Force photo by Staff Sgt. Ryan Hansen)

27 June 2006, Vandenberg AFB, California – A Boeing Delta IV carrying a payload for the National Reconnaissance Office lifts off from Space Launch Complex 6 (SLC-6), the former, never-used Space Shuttle complex. (U.S. Air Force photo by Staff Sgt. Quinton Russ)

27 June 2006, over Southwest Asia – A Boeing KC-135 Stratotanker from the 22nd Expeditionary Air Refueling Squadron from Manas Air Base, Kyrgyzstan, refuels an A-10 Thunderbolt II over Afghanistan. (U.S. Air Force photo by Airman 1st Class Lonnie Mast)

29 June 2006, Aviano Air Base, Italy – Severe thunderstorms, with wind gusts measuring up to 82 knots, caused basewide damage estimated at $3.5 million. Note the overturned H-60 Blackhawk in the center of the photo. (U.S. Air Force photo by Airman 1st Class Nathan Doza)

02 July 2006, Southwest Asia – First Lt. Benjamin Aldus inspects a GBU-12 bomb during a preflight inspection. Lieutenant Aldus is a weapons system officer with the 335th Expeditionary Fighter Squadron. (U.S. Air Force photo by Master Sgt. Dutch DeGroot)

02 July 2006, Southwest Asia – Capt. Michael Shields inspects the arming device on the ejection seat of a Boeing F-15 Eagle while Capt. Marc Johnson watches during a preflight inspection. (U.S. Air Force photo by Master Sgt. Dutch DeGroot)

03 July 2006, Southwest Asia – A Lockheed Martin M142 High-Mobility Artillery Rocket System is offloaded from a C-17 Globemaster III onto a dirt landing strip. The C-17 mission re-supplied coalition international security assistance forces in a remote region of Afghanistan. (U.S. Air Force photo by Capt. Krista Staff)

04 July 2006, Andersen AFB, Guam – The Boeing F-15E Strike Eagles are with the 391st Expeditionary Fighter Squadron from Mountain Home AFB, Idaho. The Northrop-Grumman B-2A Spirit is from the 325th Expeditionary Bomb Squadron from Whiteman AFB, Missouri. (U.S. Air Force photo by Tech. Cecilio Ricardo)

05 July 2006, Kunsan Air Base, South Korea – Tech. Sgt. Mike Geske (front) and Staff Sgt. Carl Valvota secure a Mk-82 bomb to a Lockheed Martin F-16 Fighting Falcon. The aircraft is from the New Mexico Air National Guard's 150th Fighter Wing at Albuquerque. (U.S. Air Force Photo by Tech. Sgt. Erik Gudmundson)

07 July 2006, Fort Worth, Texas – The Lockheed Martin F-35 Lightning II is presented for the first time during the inauguration ceremony at the Lockheed Martin plant in Ft. Worth. The Lightning II, formerly the Joint Strike Fighter (JSF), is a fifth-generation, supersonic stealth fighter designed to replace a wide range of existing aircraft, including the AV-8B Harrier, A-10 Thunderbolt II, F-16 Fighting Falcon, F/A-18 Hornet and Royal Air Force Harrier GR-7 and Sea Harriers. (Images courtesy of Lockheed Martin)

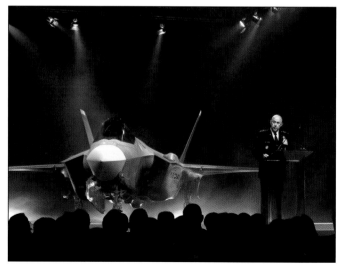

10 July 2006, RAF Lakenheath, England – A Boeing F-15E Strike Eagle, assigned to the 494th Fighter Squadron, launches on a training mission with the new BRU-61 bomb rack and GBU-39 small-diameter bombs attached to the center pylon. The aircraft was one of four to participate in the first training mission with the new weapon. (U.S. Air Force photo by Airman 1st Class Michael Hess)

08 July 2006, Balad Air Base, Iraq – MQ-1 Predator unmanned aerial vehicles from the 46th Expeditionary Strike and Reconnaissance Squadron at Nellis AFB sit ready for missions over Iraq Assigned to the 332nd Air Expeditionary Wing, the Predator is the most requested weapons system in the U.S. Central Command theater. Balad is home to the largest Predator operation in the world, providing real time "eyes in the skies" to ground commanders for identifying enemy activities. (U.S. Air Force photo by Master Sgt. Jonathan F. Doti)

06 July 2006, Bagram Air Base, Afghanistan – Capt. Jason Shemchuk exits his A-10 Warthog after a mission in support of Operation Enduring Freedom. Shemchuk is assigned to the 81st Expeditionary Fighter Squadron. (U.S. Air Force photo by Airman 1st Class Andrew Oquendo)

06 July 2006, Bagram Air Base, Afghanistan – A Fairchild-Republic/Lockheed A-10 Thunderbolt II sits on a ramp waiting for its next mission. The A-10 is used for close-air support. (U.S. Air Force photo by Airman 1st Class Andrew Oquendo)

10 July 2006, Kirkuk Air Base, Iraq – A completed Iraqi Air Force Comp Air 7SLX is prepared for a test flight. The United Arab Emirates donated several of the six-seat kit-built aircraft to the Iraqi Air Force. (U.S. Air Force photo by Staff Sgt. Stacy Fowler)

11 July 2006, New Al Muthana Air Base, Iraq – Senior Airman Jeff McCain works with the Coalition Air Force Transition Team to rebuild the Iraqi Air Force. (U.S. Air Force photo by Staff Sgt. Bryan Bouchard)

08 July 2006, Kirtland AFB, New Mexico – The Air Force Special Operations Command's new Bell CV-22 Osprey on a training flight with the 58th Special Operations Wing. (Bell Helicopter photo via the U.S. Air Force)

11 July 2006, Luke AFB, Arizona – An F-16 Fighting Falcon painted with the Tuskegee Airmen's signature red tail is lowered into place in the Tuskegee Airmen Memorial Airpark in front of the 944th Fighter Wing at Luke. (U.S. Air Force photo by Staff Sgt. Susan Stout)

16 July 2006, Hickam AFB, Hawaii – Staff Sgt. Arthur Hamabata and Staff Sgt. Gabriel Coronado load an AIM-7 Sparrow missile on a Boeing F-15 Eagle during the Rim of the Pacific Exercise 2006. The Airmen are from the Hawaii Air National Guard's 154th Aircraft Maintenance Squadron. The missiles were launched during a mass firing (below) the same day. (U.S. Air Force photo by Tech. Sgt. Shane A. Cuomo)

U.S. Air Force Aviation

18 July 2006, over Southwest Asia – A Lockheed Martin F-16 Fighting Falcon flies a close-air-support mission in support of Operation Iraqi Freedom. The F-16 is from the Alabama Air National Guard. (U.S. Air Force photo by Senior Airman Brian Ferguson)

18 July 2006, Southwest Asia – A Boeing F-15E Strike Eagle pulls up to the refueling boom of a Boeing KC-10 Extender from the 908th Expeditionary Air Refueling Squadron. (U.S. Air Force photo by Senior Airman Brian Ferguson)

18 July 2006, Eielson AFB, Alaska – Several Saab JAS 39 Gripen from the Swedish Air Force's Tango Red unit based at Malmen Air Base, Sweden, sit on the flightline at Eielson in preparation for Cooperative Cope Thunder 2006. (U.S. Air Force photo by Staff Sgt. Joshua Strang)

25 July 2006, over the North Sea – Capt. Joseph Petrosky (right) adjusts his intercom settings aboard a Boeing KC-135 Stratotanker. Captain Petrosky, an instructor pilot, mentored Capts. Rob Kline (left) and Sam Ensminger on the duties and responsibilities of being aircraft com-manders. The 351st Air Refueling Squadron aircrew launched from RAF Mildenhall, England, and refueled six Belgian Lockheed Martin F-16 Fighting Falcons over the North Sea participating in exercise Wycombe Warrior. (U.S. Air Force photo by Master Sgt. Lance Cheung)

25 July 2006, Elmendorf AFB, Alaska – Senior Airman Sherman Roberts loads liquid oxygen into a C-130 during Cooperative Cope Thunder. Roberts is with the 36th Aircraft Maintenance Unit at Yokota Air Base, Japan. (U.S. Air Force photo by Senior Airman Garrett Hothan)

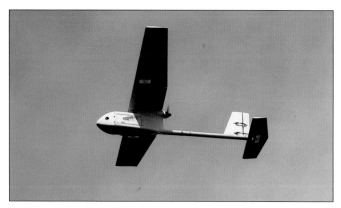

28 July 2006, Colorado Springs, Colorado – An unmanned aerial vehicle with a camera mounted on board was the focus of a Remote Operated Video Enhanced Receiver demonstration at the Air Force Academy. (U.S. Air Force photo by Dennis Rogers)

01 August 2006, RAF Lakenheath, England – Boeing F-15E Strike Eagles from the 492nd Fighter Squadron return from a two-week deployment to Graf-Isnatievo Air Base, Bulgaria, where they took part in exercise Immediate Response. Airmen from the 48th Fighter Wing provided support during the trilateral exercise with the Bulgarian and Romanian militaries. (U.S. Air Force photo by Master Sgt. Lance Cheung)

01 August 2006, RAF Lakenheath, England – Airman 1st Class James Willett (left) and Staff Sgt. David Cruz disarm an F-15E. The Airmen are weapons specialists with the 48th Aircraft Maintenance Squadron. (U.S. Air Force photo by Master Sgt. Lance Cheung)

01 August 2006, RAF Lakenheath, England – Four ground-training 250-pound GBU-39 small-diameter bombs on a BRU-61 carrier and munitions trailer. The 494th Fighter Wing will be the first unit to use the bomb when it deploys to Southwest Asia later this year. Airman 1st Class Matt Aggers and Staff Sgt. Randy Broome perform a final check of the bombs, which use a pair of wings to increase their range; the wings are shown in their stowed position. (U.S. Air Force photo by Master Sgt. Lance Cheung)

14 August 2006, over Alaska – An Air Force Boeing KC-135 Stratotanker refuels a Boeing F/A-18 Hornet from the Navy's Blue Angels demonstration team on its way from an air show at Elmendorf AFB, Alaska. The KC-135 is with the 168th Air Refueling Wing at Eielson AFB, Alaska. Note the attachment hose that allows the KC-135 to refuel Navy aircraft equipped with probe-and-drogue refueling systems instead of flying boom receptacles. (U.S. Air Force photo by Senior Airman Anthony Nelson Jr.)

14 August 2006 - McChord AFB, Washington – A 62nd Airlift Wing Boeing C-17 Globemaster III returns from Balad Air Base, Iraq. The aircraft had deployed to the 332nd Air Expeditionary Wing, the only Air Force wing in Iraq. (U.S. Air Force photo)

11 August 2006, Scott AFB, Illinois – The Thunderbird diamond formation passes in review during a practice show. The Thunderbirds have flown various models of the Lockheed Martin F-16 Fighting Falcon since 1983. (U.S. Air Force photo by Master Sgt. Jack Braden)

11 August 2006, Scott AFB, Illinois – Thunderbirds Nos. 5 and 6 perform a reflection pass during a practice show. Although the aircraft appear impossibly close together, safe separation is always maintained. (U.S. Air Force photo by Master Sgt. Jack Braden)

16 August 2006, over North Carolina – A Lockheed Martin F-22 Raptor from Nellis AFB flies over Kill Devil Hills. (U.S. Air Force photo by Tech. Sgt. Ben Bloker)

16 August 2006, Mihail Kogalniceanu Air Base, Romania – Senior Airman Richard Bates (left) and Staff Sgt. Mark Pastian download an AIM-9 training missile from an F-16 during Exercise Viper Lance 2006. (U.S. Air Force photo by Senior Airman Eydie Sakura)

18 August 2006, Mihail Kogalniceanu Air Base, Romania – (front to back) Staff Sgts. Jeremy Crombie and Brandon Holloway and Senior Airman Joshua Hood work to upload a targeting pod on an F-16 Fighting Falcon. (U.S. Air Force photo by Senior Airman Eydie Sakura)

A Boeing F-15 Eagle from the 65th Aggressor Squadron shows its new camouflage paint scheme. (U.S. Air Force photo)

18 August 2006, off the coast of South Korea – A Lockheed Martin F-16 Fighting Falcon from the 80th Fighter Squadron at Kunsan Air Base, South Korea, fires an AIM-9 missile during a live-fire exercise. (U.S. Air Force photo by Tech. Sgt. Jeffrey Allen)

18 August 2006, Southwest Asia – Maj. Jeff O'Donnell and 1st Lt. Nathan Rivinius stand by in their Boeing F-15E Strike Eagle and wait for the chocks to be pulled before a combat mission. They are deployed to the 335th Expeditionary Fighter Squadron from Seymour-Johnson AFB, North Carolina. (U.S. Air Force photo by Master Sgt. John DeGroot)

20 August 2006, over northern Minnesota – A Lockheed Martin C-130 Hercules from the Minnesota Air National Guard's 133rd Airlift Wing flies over the shore of Mille Lacs Lake during a training mission. (U.S. Air Force photo by Tech. Sgt. Erik Gudmundson)

18 August 2006, near Minot AFB, North Dakota – Missile Alert Facility (MAF) B-1 (right) is one of fifteen similar 91st Space Wing facilities scattered across northwest North Dakota. Each contains living quarters and support equipment for the facility manager, alert facility chef, and security personnel. Buried below the MAF are the equipment area and launch control center used by the missile combat crew to control and monitor Minuteman III missiles in dispersed underground launch facilities. First Lt. John Manibusan (left) and Second Lt. Trey Marshall are on duty for 24 hours, although if necessary, they can remain sealed in the capsule for a week, existing on stored food and water and relying on self-contained power and environmental systems. The officers are with the 740th Missile Squadron. (U.S. Air Force photos by Master Sgt. Lance Cheung)

20 August 2006, Minot AFB, North Dakota – The Boeing B-52H Stratofortress is still one of the most capable heavy bombers in the inventory. Below, operators Capt. Jeff Rogers (left) and 1st Lt. Patrick Applegate. (U.S. Air Force photos by Master Sgt. Lance Cheung)

22 August 2006, Dover AFB, Delaware – The flight deck from a Lockheed Martin C-5 Galaxy that crashed near Dover on 3 April is loaded aboard another C-5. Below, Airmen 1st Class Ryan Harrison and Jamie Abernathy and Staff Sgt. Stuard Smith tie down the salvaged crew compartment which will be used as a simulator to help train and test aircrews. (U.S. Air Force photo by Airman 1st Class James Bolinger)

23 August 2006, over Nevada – An F-16 flies in formation with a KC-135 after being refueled during Red Flag 06-2. The refueling track is about 100 miles northeast of Nellis, near the Utah border. (U.S. Air Force photo by Airman 1st Class Andrew Dumboski)

23 August 2006, over Nevada – A Lockheed Martin F-16 Fighting Falcon from Misawa Air Base, Japan, pulls away from a KC-135 Stratotanker from MacDill AFB, during Red Flag 06-2. (U.S. Air Force Photo by Senior Airman Travis Edwards)

25 August 2006, Shaw AFB, South Carolina – An F-16 Fighting Falcon from the 79th Fighter Squadron engages the aircraft barrier during a certification test. The barrier is used during emergency landings. (U.S. Air Force photo by Airman Matthew Davis)

24 August 2006, over Nevada – a Boeing F-15 Eagle from Kadena Air Base, Japan, pulls away from a Boeing KC-135 Stratotanker after refueling during Red Flag, a two-week exercise that tests and trains servicemembers in real-time combat situations. Red Flag is conducted over the Nevada Test and Training Range, which has more than 2.9 million acres of airspace. The KC-135 is based at MacDill AFB, Florida. (U.S. Air Force photo by Senior Airman Travis Edwards)

29 August 2006, over the Sea of Japan – Pararescuemen from the 31st Rescue Squadron perform a static-line jump out of a Lockheed Martin C-130 Hercules near Kadena Air Base, Japan. The 18th Wing and the 353rd Special Operations Group conducted an exercise to test their rescue and emergency care capabilities. (U.S. Air Force photo by Staff Sgt. Steven Nabor)

29 August 2006, Kadena Air Base, Japan – Airmen from the 18th Aeromedical Evacuation Squadron aboard a Lockheed Martin C-130 Hercules care for a simulated patient during a mass casualty exercise. (U.S. Air Force photo by Staff Sgt. Steven Nabor)

25 August 2006, over Fort Irwin, California – Joint Precision Air Drop System bundles fall out of the back of a Lockheed Martin C-130 Hercules. The drop was made from 10,000 feet altitude. (U.S. Air Force photo by Senior Airman Brian Ferguson)

30 August 2006, Andersen AFB, Guam – This 23rd Expeditionary Bomb Squadron Boeing B-52 Stratofortress from the 5th Bomb Wing at Minot AFB is one of six deployed to Andersen for four months. (U.S. Air Force photo by Airman 1st Class Miranda Moorer)

01 September 2006, over Nevada – 414th Combat Training Squadron Pararescuemen and parachutists from the 820th Red Horse Squadron at Nellis AFB jump out of a C-130J Hercules. (U.S. Air Force photo by Master Sgt. Kevin J. Gruenwald)

06 September 2006, Ramstein Air Base, Germany – A 60-ton Netherlander Howitzer 2000 is fastened to the floor of a Boeing C-17 Globemaster III for a trip to Afghanistan. (U.S. Air Force photo by Master Sgt. John Lasky)

09 September 2006, St. Louis, Missouri – A Northrop-Grumman B-2 Spirit stealth bomber sits on the tarmac at the 131st Fighter Wing at Lambert International Airport. (U.S. Air Force photo by Master Sgt. Mary-Dale Amison)

12 September 2006, approaching Wake Island – Maj. Joseph Golovach and Capt. John Ramsey III bring their Boeing C-17 Globemaster III in for a landing with a 53-person team to assess damage left by Super Typhoon Loke after it struck the island on 31 August. Both pilots are from the 535th Airlift Squadron at Hickam AFB, Hawaii. (U.S. Air Force photo by Tech. Sgt. Shane A. Cuomo)

12 September 2006, Bagram Air Base, Afghanistan – Tech. Sgt. Michael Leach and Staff Sgt. Gordon Torrey drive a "follow-me" to its parking spot. The C-17, from the 62nd Airlift Wing at McChord AFB, Washington, was the 2,000th transient aircraft to land at Bagram for Air Expeditionary Forces 1 and 2, which began 7 May. That equates to an average of 17 aircraft transiting Bagram daily. (U.S. Air Force photo by Maj. David Kurle)

19 September 2006, Lackland AFB, Texas – The first Lockheed Martin C-130 Hercules modified by Boeing under the C-130 Avionics Modernization Program takes off on its initial test flight. The modifications include a comprehensive upgrade of the avionics system that increases situational awareness for the flight crew ten-fold over old analog cockpits, dramatically increasing information available to aircrews at a glance, simplifying tasks, and decreasing workload. (Boeing photo via the U.S. Air Force)

16 September 2006, Davis-Monthan AFB, Arizona – Capt. Joseph Hext (in cockpit) of the 354th Fighter Squadron performs a pre-flight check on his A-10 Thunderbolt II during exercise Bushwacker 06-04. (U.S. Air Force photo by Senior Airman Jesse Shipps)

18 September 2006, Andersen AFB, Guam – Tech. Sgt. Timothy Scheaffer prepares to do engine work on a Boeing B-52 Stratofortress, illustrating the size of the Pratt & Whitney TF33 turbofan engines. (U.S. Air Force photo by Marine Cpl. Ashleigh Bryant)

20 September 2006, Hickam AFB, Hawaii – Airmen from the 15th Airlift Wing wait to board an Indian Air Force Ilyushin IL-76 Candid medium cargo aircraft for a training mission with a visiting Indian aircrew. (U.S. Air Force photo by Tech. Sgt. Shane A. Cuomo)

20 September 2006, Balad Air Base, Iraq – Weapons loaders from the 332nd Expeditionary Aircraft Maintenance Squadron wait outside a hardened shelter before loading a Lockheed Martin F-16 Fighting Falcon. (U.S. Air Force photo by Senior Airman Kerry Solan-Johnson)

21 September 2006, Southwest Asia – Staff Sgt. Sean Tracey, Senior Airman Sean Timothy and Airman 1st Class Henry Rodriguez perform a post-flight inspection on a Boeing F-15 Strike Eagle. (U.S. Air Force photo by Master Sgt. Scott Wagers)

28 September 2006, near Alaska – A Boeing F-15C Eagle from the 12th Fighter Squadron at Elmendorf AFB flies next to a Russian Air Force Tupolev Tu-95 Bear bomber during a Russian exercise near the west coast of Alaska. (U.S. Air Force photo)

22 September 2006, San Diego, California – Airmen prepare a CV-22 Osprey for a training exercise with Navy Seals at Naval Air Station North Island, California. (U.S. Navy photo by Mass Communication Specialist Daniel A. Barker)

15 October 2006, over New Mexico – The Bell CV-22 Osprey fills a long-standing U.S. Special Operations Command requirement to conduct long-range infiltration, exfiltration, and resupply missions. (U.S. Air Force photo by Tech Sgt. Cecilio M. Ricardo Jr.)

02 October 2006, Southwest Asia – Senior Airman Jered Danielson pauses to review a checklist before crawling into the boom control station of a Boeing KC-135R Stratotanker. (U.S. Air Force photo by Master Sgt. D. Scott Wagers)

15 October 2006, Kadena Air Base, Japan – Senior Airmen James White and Robert Crothers inspect one of two Pratt & Whitney F100 engines from a Boeing F-15 Eagle during routine maintenance. (U.S. Air Force photo by Airman Kelly Timney)

12 October 2006, Columbus AFB, Mississippi – Lt. Col. Todd White taxies the first T-6 Texan assigned to Columbus before presenting it to Col. Eric Theisen, commander of the 41st Flying Training Squadron. (U.S. Air Force photo by Senior Airman Cecilia Rodriguez)

30 September 2006, over Southern California – Scaled Composites Proteus makes the first flight of the Global Hawk variant of the new Multi-Platform Radar Technology Insertion Program radar. (Photo courtesy of Northrop Grumman)

13 October 2006, Arlington, Virginia – A Bell CV-22 Osprey tilt-rotor aircraft lands at the Pentagon. A variety of aircraft, including a CV-22, were put on display during the Air Force open house for the opening ceremonies of the Air Force Memorial (facing page) on 14 October. Unlike most memorials in the Nation's capitol, the Air Force Memorial is in Virginia on a hill overlooking Arlington National Cemetery and the Pentagon. (U.S. Air Force photo by Master Sgt. Gary R. Coppage)

13 October 2006, Arlington, Virginia – A Bell CV-22 Osprey hovers over the new Air Force Memorial with the Pentagon in the background. *The Memorial was dedicated on 14 October.* (U.S. Air Force photo by Master Sgt. Gary R. Coppage)

14 October 2006, Arlington, Virginia – *Designed by the late James Ingo Freed, the spires of the Air Force Memorial were inspired by the U.S. Air Force Thunderbirds "bomb burst" maneuver.* (U.S. Air Force photo by Tech. Sgt. Christopher J. Matthews)

13 October 2006, Beale AFB, California – Avionics specialists with the 12th Aircraft Maintenance Unit prepare a Northrop-Grumman RQ-4 Global Hawk for a taxi test. The Global Hawk is scheduled to begin flying at Beale in early November. The program is a total force effort with the Air Force Reserve's 13th Reconnaissance Squadron assisting active duty personnel. (U.S. Air Force photo by Stacey Knott)

15 October 2006, over Turkey – A Lockheed Martin F-16 Fighting Falcon performs combat air patrol over the glaciers of central Turkey during Exercise Anatolian Eagle. (U.S. Air Force photo by Master Sgt. Ron Przysucha)

17 October 2006, over Iraq – A Boeing KC-10 Extender connects to a second KC-10 from the 380th Air Expeditionary Wing. It is not unusual for tankers to refuel other tankers to extend the range of strike aircraft. (U.S. Air Force photo by Staff Sgt. Nicholas Jacobson)

16 October 2006, Marietta, Georgia – Lockheed Martin rolls out the first combat-capable F-22 Raptor stealth fighter destined for the Pacific Theater at Elmendorf AFB, Alaska. The aircraft will receive its final paint and radar absorbent coating after an initial round of ground testing. (Lockheed Martin photo via the U.S. Air Force)

19 October 2006, Nellis AFB, Nevada – A Lockheed Martin F-16 Fighting Falcon takes off, while other aircraft go through pre-flight checks during Red Flag 07-1. F-15 and F-16 aggressors are in the background. (U.S. Air Force photo by Master Sgt. Kevin J. Gruenwald)

19 October 2006, Nellis AFB, Nevada – A Boeing F-15C Eagle is parked on the flight line during Red Flag 07-1. The aircraft fly missions day and night to the nearby Nevada Test and Training Range. (U.S. Air Force photo by Airman First Class Brian Ybarbo)

18 October 2006, Nellis AFB, Nevada – A Boeing F-15C Eagle aggressor from the 65th Aggressor Squadron shows off its new desert camouflage during Red Flag 07-1 (exercises are numbered based on fiscal years, which begin in October). (U.S. Air Force photo)

28 October 2006, Davis-Monthan AFB, Arizona – Senior Airmen Randy Loera (left) and Jesse Vida install chaff and flare dispensers under the wingtip of a Fairchild-Republic/Lockheed A-10 Thunderbolt II. Additional dispensers are located on the main landing gear fairings. The Airmen are weapons loaders from the 355th Maintenance Operations Squadron. (U.S. Air Force photo by A1C Alesia Goosic)

23 October 2006, over Southwest Asia – After taking on fuel from a Boeing KC-135 Stratotanker four miles above Iraq, a Lockheed Martin F-16 Fighting Falcon deployed from Canon AFB, New Mexico, pulls away to resume its close-air support mission for coalition forces on the ground. (U.S. Air Force photo by Master Sgt. Scott Wagers)

01 November 2006, Travis AFB, California – Master Sgt. Etsuro Mizokami from the Japan Air Self Defense Force practices refueling an aircraft in a simulator at Travis. Japan is taking delivery of three Boeing KC-767 tankers, and Mizokami is one of the first three Japanese boom operators. (U.S. Air Force photo)

27 October 2006, Holloman AFB, New Mexico – Senior Airman Francisco Pio and Staff Sgt. Joseph Metoyer from the 49th Aircraft Maintenance Squadron at Holloman finish an end of runway check. The F-117 was one of 25 Nighthawks to fly in a formation celebrating the aircraft's 25th anniversary. (U.S. Air Force photo by Senior Airman Brian Ferguson)

05 November 2006, Lackland AFB, Texas – The U. S. Air Force Thunderbirds take off for their final 2006 road show performance at Lackland AFB. An estimated crowd of 250,00 attended the two-day air show. (U.S. Air Force photo)

04 November 2006, McConnell AFB, Kansas – A Boeing C-17 Globemaster III, belonging to 62nd Airlift Wing at McChord AFB, Washington, is loaded in preparation for a mission to Southwest Asia. (U.S. Air Force photo by Navy Petty Officer 2nd Class Troy Karr)

28 October 2006, Charleston AFB, South Carolina – President George W. Bush delivers a speech in front of several Boeing C-17 Globemaster IIIs and more than 4,000 servicemembers and families. The ceremony was part of a rally to support for the wars in Southwest Asia. (U.S. Air Force photo by Tech. Sgt. Larry A. Simmons)

14 November 2006, Misawa Air Base, Japan – Lt. Col. Andrew Dembosky climbs into his Lockheed Martin F-16 Fighting Falcon as Crew Chief Staff Sgt. Robert Parsons helps with the preflight preparations. (U.S. Air Force photo by Senior Airman Robert Barnett)

19 November 2006, Southwest Asia – Staff Sgt. James Parker runs to the middle of the taxiway to martial a Boeing RC-135 Rivet Joint reconnaissance aircraft for a mission over Southwest Asia. (U.S. Air Force photo by Master Sgt. Scott Wagers)

10 November 2006, over the Idaho Sawtooth Mountains – (above and top of facing page) Colonel Anthony Rock, 366th Fighter Wing commander, led this five-ship formation of two Boeing F-15E Strike Eagles, a Boeing F-15C Eagle, and a Lockheed Martin F-16C Fighting Falcon, all from the 366th Fighter Wing at Mountain Home AFB, Idaho, and a Northrop-Grumman EA-6B Prowler from the 388th Electronic Control Squadron at NAS Whidbey Island, Washington. The 388th ECS is tasked to man, train, and equip Air Force aircrew to employ expeditionary U.S. Navy EA-6Bs. (U.S. Air Force photo by Master Sgt. Kevin J. Gruenwald)

20 November 2006, over Turkey – Colonel Darryl Roberson flies his F-16 Fighting Falcon over the Turkish mountains after completing the final mission of Exercise Anatolian Eagle at Konya Air Base, Turkey. (U.S. Air Force photo by Master Sgt. Ron Przysucha)

20 November 2006, over Iraq – An F-16 from Balad Air Base takes fuel from a KC-10 Extender in support of Operation Iraqi Freedom. The KC-10 aircrew is deployed in support of the 380th Air Expeditionary Wing. (U.S. Air Force photo by Capt. Justin T. Watson)

21 November 2006, Manas Air Base, Kyrgyzstan – Senior Airman Ryan Saunders blasts the snow and ice off a KC-135 Stratotanker prior to the aircraft's next mission over Afghanistan. (U.S. Air Force photo by Master Sgt. Mitch Gettle)

30 November 2006, over Iraq – An E-8C Joint STARS aircraft departs from a deployed location in Southwest Asia. The flight over Iraq marked 20,000 flying hours in support of Operation Iraqi Freedom. (U.S. Air Force photo by Senior Airman Ricky Best)

12 November 2006, Nellis AFB, Nevada – A General Atomics RQ-1 Predator with two AGM-114 Hellfire missiles. The Predator has proven very effective in Southwest Asia and is the darling of the popular news media. (U.S. Air Force photo)

02 November 2006, Kunsan Air Base, Korea – A Lockheed Martin F-16 Fighting Falcon takes off on a training mission. Aircraft are always at the ready, flying training missions around the clock to ensure total readiness. (U.S. Air Force photo)

05 November 2006, over Southwest Asia – A Royal Air Force Tornado strike aircraft prepares to connect with the trailing drogue of a Boeing KC-10 Extender over Iraq. (U.S. Air Force photo by Capt. Justin T. Watson)

02 November 2006, Andersen AFB, Guam – Staff Sgt. Joshua Sweet (below, right) guides Airman 1st Class Wayne Robinson as he positions an Mk-56 mine under the wing of a Boeing B-52H Stratofortress. Staff Sgt. Jason Smith (on ladder) and Sergeant Sweet will secure the weapon once it is in position. Above, the B-52 takes off armed with four Mk-56 mines on the tenth and final mission of a week-long joint sea mine-laying exercise with the Navy. The B-52s dropped a total of 96 inert mines on two practice mine fields that were each three miles long and a mile wide. (U.S. Air Force photos by Staff Sgt. Eric Petosky)

06 November 2006, Hurlburt Field, Florida – Airman 1st Class Joshua Penery (left to right), Senior Airman Cody Husemann, Airman 1st Class Jeffrey Miller and Airman 1st Class Steven Bickell, members of the 16th Special Operations Wing Honor Guard, perform in front of a Bell CV-22 Osprey. The commemoration was marked by the arrival of the CV-22 to Hurlburt Field and the redesignation of Air Force Special Operations Command's 16th Special Operations Wing as the 1st SOW. (U.S. Air Force photo by Chief Master Sgt. Gary Emery)

12 November 2006, Nellis AFB, Nevada – The United States Air Force demonstration team, the Thunderbirds, perform maneuvers during the last air show of the 2006 tour season, (U.S Air Force Photo by Staff Sgt Jeremy Smith)

14 November 2006, Antarctica – Senior Airman Kory Williams, 8th Airlift Squadron, and Senior Master Sgt. David Stutts, 313th Airlift Squadron, assess a C-17 after landing on the ice at McMurdo Station, Antarctica. (U.S. Air Force photo by 1st Lt Erika Yepsen)

06 November 2006, Hurlburt Field, Florida – Airman 1st Class Stephen Emminger, a security response team member with the 16th Security Forces Squadron, guards Air Force Special Operations Command's first operational Bell CV-22 Osprey. The Osprey was flown to Hurlburt by Lt. Gen. Michael W. Wooley, AFSOC commander, as part of the command's Air Force 60th anniversary commemoration. (U.S. Air Force photo by Chief Master Sgt. Gary Emery)

14 November 2006, Antarctica – Cargo is transported from a Boeing C-17 Globemaster III from McChord AFB to an awaiting Lockheed Martin LC-130 Hercules operated by the New York Air National Guard near McMurdo Station, Antarctica. The LC-130 is equipped with skis to aid in landing on the snow and ice, but the C-17 is not and requires a relatively firm ice runway to be available. Flights can only be made during the short summer months. (U.S. Air Force photo by 1st Lt Erika Yepsen)

16 November 2006, Hurlburt Field, Florida – A Bell CV-22 Osprey flies over the flightline. (U.S. Air Force photo by Senior Airman Ali E. Flisek)

13 November 2006, Incirlik Air Base, Turkey – Airmen from the 728th Airlift Wing load a Boeing C-17 Globemaster III. Over half of all air cargo delivered to support Operation Iraqi Freedom is processed through Incirlik. By flying critical supplies via Globemaster from Turkey directly to troops at remote locations in Iraq, more than 3,300 convoy truck missions and 9,000 servicemembers to support the convoys are taken off the Iraqis roads each month. (U.S. Air Force photo by Tech. Sgt. Larry A. Simmons)

19 November 2006, Southwest Asia – A Boeing RC-135 Rivet Joint reconnaissance aircraft, with CFM F108 (CFM56) turbofan engines, is towed by Staff Sgt. John Terlaje and Airman 1st Class Ross Vandenbosch. (U.S. Air Force photo by Master Sgt. Scott Wagers)

19 November 2006, Southwest Asia – Senior Airman Matthew Campbell and Airman 1st Class Jonathan Campana remove one of many air conditioning hoses on an RC-135 Rivet Joint reconnaissance aircraft. (U.S. Air Force photo by Master Sgt. Scott Wagers)

19 November 2006, Southwest Asia – Airman Mark Magill inspects the number two F108-model high bypass turbofan on an RC-135. The engine was introduced to the 135-airframe in August 1998. (U.S. Air Force photo by Master Sgt. Scott Wagers)

19 November 2006, Southwest Asia – Air conditioning hoses help maintain cool temperatures for the extensive inventory of electronics aboard the RC-135 during its lengthy pre-flight process. (U.S. Air Force photo by Master Sgt. Scott Wagers)

21 November 2006, Southwest Asia – An Army H-60 Blackhawk heli-copter touches down near the Balad Air Base runway in the final minutes of sunlight delivered by a setting Iraqi sunset. (U.S. Air Force photo by Master Sgt. Scott Wagers)

02 December 2006, Southwest Asia – Senior Airman Matthew Turner with the 379th Logistics Readiness Squadron, monitors the outgoing fuel pressure on an R11 fuel truck feeding a Boeing KC-135 Stratotanker. (U.S. Air Force photo by MSgt Scott Wagers)

28 November 2006, Southwest Asia – A Lockheed Martin F-16 from Balad Air Base takes fuel from a Boeing KC-10 Extender over Iraq. The KC-10 aircrew is deployed in support of the 380th Air Expeditionary Wing. (U.S. Air Force photo by Capt. Justin T. Watson)

29 November 2006, Davis-Monthan AFB, Arizona – A newly arrived A-10C Thunderbolt II has been modified with new sensors, multi-functional color displays, and a hands-on-throttle-and-stick inter-face. (U.S. Air Force photo by Airman 1st Class Alesia Goosic)

14 December 2006, Southwest Asia – An A-10 Thunderbolt II pulls away after receiving fuel from a KC-10 Extender flying over Afghanistan. The tanker is from the 380th Air Expeditionary Wing, home of the largest air refueling wing in Southwest Asia. Note the shark-mouth on the A-10 – a favorite motif since the late 1930s. (U.S. Air Force photo by Capt. Justin T. Watson)

15 December 2006, Tullahoma, Tennessee – Tim Wright examines an F-35 LIghtning II Joint Strike Fighter model in the Arnold Engineering Development Center 16-foot transonic wind tunnel. The information from testing will go into a database to refine and validate the aircraft designs prior to flight testing. (U.S. Air Force photo by David Housch)

08 December 2006, over Nevada – 820th Civil Engineering Red Horse personnel and Army Airborne prepare to exit a Boeing C-17 Globemaster III during a mission employment exercise held at Nellis AFB. (U.S. Air Force photo by Master. Sgt. Kevin J. Gruenwald)

15 December 2006, over the South Pacific – The boom from a Boeing KC-135 Stratotanker operated by the 434th Air Refueling Wing is visible as the aircraft flies over Wake Island. (U.S. Air Force photo by Tech. Sgt. Shane A. Cuomo)

15 December 2006, Fort Worth, Texas – The Lockheed Martin F-35 Lightning II Joint Strike Fighter makes its initial flight from the Lockheed Martin facility at Carswell Joint Reserve Base. (Lockheed Martin photos by David Drais and Tom Harvey)

11 December 2006, Arlington National Cemetery, Virginia – Members of the Caisson Platoon of the 3rd U.S. Infantry, The Old Guard, carry Major Troy Gilbert to his grave site. Major Gilbert was the pilot of an F-16 that crashed approximately 20 miles northwest of Baghdad on 27 November. Gilbert was assigned to the 309th Fighter Squadron, Luke AFB, Arizona, and was deployed to the 332nd Expeditionary Wing, Balad Air Base, Iraq. (U.S. Air Force photo)